T

j
818.5
MICHAEL
1992

102
Creepy, Crawly
Bug Jokes

by Ski Michaels

Troll

Walla Walla
County Libraries

D0019067

Library of Congress Cataloging-in-Publication Data

Michaels, Ski.
  102 creepy, crawly bug jokes / by Ski Michaels.
    p.   cm.
  Summary: Includes "What do you call a newborn ant? A baby buggy."
and "Which bug costs only a penny? The cent-i-pede."
  ISBN 0-8167-2745-7 (pbk.)
  1. Wit and humor, Juvenile.   2. Insects—Juvenile humor.
[1. Insects—Wit and humor.   2. Jokes.]   I. Title.   II. Title: One
hundred and two creepy, crawly bug jokes.
PN6163.M52   1992
818'.5402—dc20   91-42737

Copyright © 1992 by Troll Communications L.L.C.

All rights reserved. No part of this book may be used or

reproduced in any manner whatsoever without written

permission from the publisher.

Printed in the United States of America.

10   9   8   7   6   5   4

Who brings colored eggs to insects?

The Easter Buggy.

What do you call a bug with a sore throat?

A hoarse fly (horsefly).

What has fins and buzzes?

A fish gnat (fish net).

**What's the best way to get rid of
unwanted insects?**

Tell them to bug off!

What kind of bugs get splinters?

Termites.

How many ants can live in an apartment?

Ten ants.

How do you keep a bug from getting cold?

Use *anti*freeze.

What do you call a newborn ant?

A baby buggy.

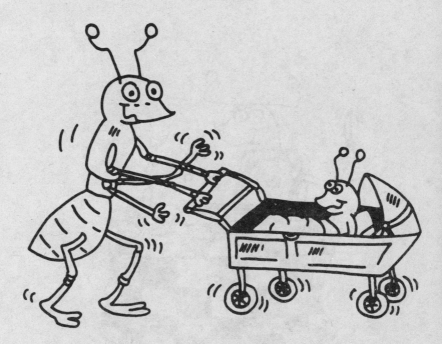

What kind of insect likes to take photographs?

A shutterbug.

Which appetizer do bugs eat?

*Ant*ipasto.

Which spider wrote a dictionary?

*Web*ster.

Which sport do insects play in England?

Rug*bee.*

Which bug jumps over cups?

The glasshopper.

What kind of cap does a bug wear?

A *bee*nie.

What happened when the bee telephoned his friend?

He got a buzzy signal.

Which bug was Robin Hood's friend?

*Fly*er (Friar) Tuck.

What does an anteater drink when it has a stomachache?

*Ant*acid.

Which line did Bugsy Shakespeare write?

"To bee or gnat to be."

Why did Princess Fly scream?

She saw a dragonfly approaching.

What goes boing! boing! boing! splat?

A grasshopper crossing a busy street.

Which dance do spiders do in Hawaii?

The Taran*thula*.

What kind of mattress does the ruler of a beehive sleep on?

Queen size.

What do you find at the end of a bug's foot?

Mosqui*toes.*

What do you find in a spider's baseball glove?

Lots of webbing.

What is the silliest bug?

The cuckoo roach (cockroach).

Which bug do you find in churches?

The praying mantis.

What do you get if you cross margarine with a bug?

A *butter*fly.

Which bugs should you hire to build a house?

Carpenter ants.

Who are the rulers of the insect kingdom?

The Queen Bee and the Monarch Butterfly.

What do you find near the top of flea shirts?

Flea collars.

What do you call two spiders who just got married?

Newlywebs.

Where did Little Bug stay while his parents went on vacation?

He stayed with his Ant (aunt).

Why did Mr. Spider go to the men's department?

To buy some pants with flies in them.

Which bug was a famous painter?

Rembr*ant*.

What do student fleas scribble notes on?

Scratch pads.

How can you tell if a dog has artistic fleas?

If he has artistic fleas, he'll always be etching.

Which bug group sings rap music?

Vanilla Lice.

What did the bug crook say when he saw the bee police?

"Scram! Here comes the buzz!"

Where does a clown bug work?

At the flea circus.

Which insects crawl and have pillows and sheets on them?

Bed bugs.

What did the firefly say to his girlfriend?

"You light up my life."

What flies and goes bizt! bizt?

A bee with a broken buzzer.

Which bug cooks greasy food?

The butter*fry.*

What did one bug say to the other?

"Hey, pal! What rock did you crawl out from under?"

What goes buzz! buzz! trip! oof?

A stumble bee.

Where does a traveling bug spend the night?

At a roach motel.

Why was Father Centipede so upset?

All of his kids needed new shoes.

Which bug has a roof and a chimney?

The housefly.

What's made of leather and has laces and wings?

A shoe fly.

Why was the farmer so upset?

He had ants in his plants.

What did the flea foreman shout to his crew?

Let's hop to it, guys!

What lives in a swamp and has lots of children?

Masquito.

What crawls and wears uniforms and helmets?

Army ants.

Why was the firefly flashing on and off?

His light was on the blink.

What goes clump! clump! clump! ouch?

A centipede stubbing its toe.

**What do you call money saved by a
stinging insect?**

A hornet's nest egg.

Why did the spider go to the baseball field?

To catch some flies in the outfield.

Which bug can tell your fortune?

The gypsy moth.

How do you keep a baby bug from getting a rash?

Use flea powder.

RATTLE!
RATTLE!

What kind of bugs live in clocks?

Ticks.

Why did the spider like eating at the cheap restaurant?

He always found a fly in his soup.

Which bugs are very nervous?

Fleas. They're always jumpy.

What did the keeper say to his swarming insects?

"Beehive (behave) yourselves."

How did the police scare the bugs away?

They called for a S.W.A.T. team.

How do bugs get rid of bad breath?

They gargle with *ant*iseptic.

In which bug sport do players dribble and shoot baskets?

Bee-ball.

Why did the little bug get sent to his room?

He was gnatty (naughty) all day.

How do insects keep their wings styled?

They use bug spray.

What happens when you play checkers with a flea?

He jumps you.

Why was the bee so sad?

He found out he was allergic to pollen.

What do corn spiders make?

Cobwebs.

Which bug works for the C.I.A.?

The *spy*der.

**What do you get if you cross a bug with an
orange?**

Beetlejuice.

Which bug starred in the movie *Raiders of the Lost Ark?*

Indi*an*ta Jones.

Why didn't the scientist demonstrate his insect invention?

He was still getting the bugs out of it.

What does a hornet wear when it's cold outside?

A yellow jacket.

What kind of insect has four wheels and a trunk?

A Volkswagen beetle.

How did the bug find a job?

He looked in the want ads of the fly paper.

Where did Jack and Jill Bug go to fetch a pail of water?

Up an anthill.

What do you call a lady spider who never gets married?

A *spin*ster.

Which pass route did the football spider run?

A fly pattern.

Which insect is always polite?

The ladybug.

Which bug do you see right before you hear thunder?

A lightning bug.

What does a clumsy grasshopper wear on his feet?

Clodhoppers.

**What do you call a big fight between winged
bugs?**

A moth brawl.

How does Dr. Insect treat a rash?

He puts a fly in the ointment.

Which bug purrs a lot?

The *cat*erpillar.

Which insects bugged King Arthur?

Fly by knights.

Which bug should you always spray with water?

The firefly.

Which bug is hot and difficult to handle?

A 3-alarm firefly.

What happens when a flea loses its temper?

It gets hopping mad.

Which insect always marries early in the summer?

The June bug.

Which bug only costs a penny?

The *cent*ipede.

Which bug likes to hit baseballs?

The batterfly (butterfly).

**What did the bee say when he saw
the honeycomb?**

"Home sweet home!"

Which spider got stuck in the road?

The *Tar*antula.

What goes drip! drip! drip! when it crawls?

A water bug.

Why did Mrs. Spider name her son Ducky?

He had webbed feet.

Why did the farmer plant bugs in his fields?

He wanted an ant farm.

What do all police bugs carry in the summer?

Tick kits (tickets).

What did the bee say when he went into the hive?

"Gee, it's swarm in here."

Walla Walla
County Libraries

What do you call bugs that wear traditional Scottish attire?

*Kilt*er bees!